POSTSCRIPT BOOKS. Edinburgh,

# PORTRAIT OF THE
# EDEN VALLEY

GRAHAM UNEY

HALSGROVE

First published in Great Britain in 2008

British Library Cataloguing-in-Publication Data
**A CIP record for this title is available from the British Library**

ISBN 978 1 84114 726 0

Halsgrove House
Ryelands Industrial Estate, Bagley Road,
Wellington, Somerset TA21 9PZ
Tel: 01823 653777
Fax: 01823 216796
email: sales@halsgrove.com
website: www.halsgrove.com

Printed and bound by Grafiche Flaminia, Italy

# INTRODUCTION

A few hundred yards west of the summit cairn of Hugh Seat, a mighty river begins its long and tumultuous journey to the sea. Hugh Seat itself is not a particularly exciting hill, but has the distinction of having three important rivers rising about its flanks.

The River Ure begins lower down, off the western rim of the plateau, taking a bending curve westwards, then south and eventually eastwards through Wensleydale in the Yorkshire Dales, onwards through the Vale of York, then out into the Humber Estuary and the North Sea.

The River Swale has a similar journey to make before its fresh, peat-stained waters can mingle with the salty, silty flats of the North Sea. It starts to the east of the summit of Hugh Seat, carving a trench to the north of Great Shunner Fell before making its mark in Swaledale, then on to join the Ure near York.

These two great rivers deserve books of their own, but this collection of photographs is focused on the third of these mighty water courses – the River Eden.

High on the open, windswept, and breathtaking moor of Hugh Seat, 2260 feet higher than the Solway Firth, way off to the north-west, Lady's Pillar stands on a heathery knoll. The pillar was erected in 1664 by Lady Anne Clifford in memory of Sir Hugh Morville, and today it can still be seen as a lichen encrusted cairn.

A short moorland walk away to the north you'll find Eden Springs. The becks here are sluggish at first, tumbling in an ungainly manner across the moorland plateau. They seem to have to force a way through the peaty morass in order to make any headway. Red Gill is the name given to the water that flows from Eden Springs, and this little beck changes in name countless times as it gains in girth and weight, feeling gravity's pull on its long downhill journey to the Solway Firth.

The infant Eden flounders across Black Fell Moss, through a landscape seemingly devoid of life and interest, but full of names redolent of the harshness through which it flows. Names like Burnt Crag, Scarth of Scaiths, Black Paddock, and Black Gutter. The infant Eden splutters and stutters across these untamed moors, passing places with names such as Sour Hill, Black Hill, and Far Capple Mere, then merrily throws itself off a brief cliff at Hell Gill Bridge. Well, with that kind of upbringing, who could blame it?

A short dash down from Hell Gill Bridge, twisting a tortuous course through the rough grasslands of the fell, there is another short shock in store for the River Eden. Hellgill Force is the first major waterfall along the course of this mighty river. There's a public bridlepath where the occasional walker will let his booted feet splash by just feet away from the crag over which the river plunges. Down it falls in sheets of spray, into a dark cavernous bowl, walls decorated with verdant mosses, liverworts, and ferns, each greenly glistening in this humid, sheltered place.

Already the Eden has gained considerably in girth and can be called a river without any stretch of the imagination. Here, just below the tumbling mass of water at the Force, the Eden turns northwards for the first time. It picks up peat and silt from the surrounding land, gathering more water from other becks and gills as it rushes onwards, headlong between the great fells of Mallerstang. To the east of the Eden these fells roll along over the scarred length of Mallerstang Edge – High Seat, Archy Styrigg, and Hugh Seat, while to the west the dale has as its enclosing wall the broad swell of Swarth Fell, and the sharp, stark outline of Wild Boar Fell.

Wildlife abounds here. Dippers find nesting caves behind white-topped stoppers in the water course, while grey wagtails flit along from boulder to boulder. In the summer months common sandpipers arrive from foreign climes and nest along its shingle banks.

And on the River Eden flows. Past Pendragon Castle beneath Little Fell.

It's nothing more than a small ruin today, but Pendragon is famous nevertheless. It was built by Henry II, and later came under the ownership of Lady Anne Clifford. Legend has it that Uther Pendragon, King Arthur's father, once held the castle. The setting itself is by far the most remarkable thing here today, especially the rough sweep of fellside that is Mallerstang Edge, dramatically carving the skyline along the east side of the dale.

By the time the Eden reaches Kirkby Stephen it is a proper, full-fledged river. The town itself turns its back on the gushing course, as the river turns withershins around the old stone houses, and ducks first beneath Frank's Bridge and then Lowmill Bridge a little further on.

Beyond Kirkby Stephen, and for the first time in its life, The River Eden has a confluence with another river, the River Belah. The Swindale Beck and Scandal Beck also merge with the main river within a distance of a mile or so of the confluence with the Belah, adding more weight and more clout to the eroding properties of the Eden.

The valley itself opens out here, though not exactly leaving the high fells behind, for further downstream the Eden will pass between the highest and grandest fells of the Pennines - Cross Fell, Great Dun Fell and Little Dun Fell, and the Northern Fells of the Lake District. It passes between these, rather than squeezes through, for the Eden Valley is now very wide indeed, and holds some sizeable towns.

The river pushes through the fertile, silty lands of the middle Eden Valley, mundifying the land, scouring the banks and the broad flood plains as it scythes in half the town of Appleby-in-Westmorland. Houses of red Penrith fell sandstone turn their backs on the often raging torrent, that is sometimes no more than a gently flowing brook.

On again the river flows, in broad, sweeping meanders, bypassing the town of Penrith itself in favour of the lower lands that lie between the villages of Langwathby, Great Salkeld and Lazonby. The river here still has a fair amount of altitude - two hundred and fifty feet or so above sea level, and not much horizontal distance in which to lose it before hitting the saltwater on the Solway Forth. It cuts a deep gorge through the soft, friable sandstone, the rock itself the bed of an ancient sea. The river gorge is the perfect place for oak and beech woodlands to flourish, and birds, badgers and deer find shelter within its confines. Red squirrels cling to the trees, themselves clinging to the slopes of the gorge, while vivid kingfishers balance easily on wispy branches overhanging the black pools of the river.

The river here looks the colour of a good strong ale or porter - perhaps Black Dub, from the nearby Geltsdale Brewery. It is the peat that has stained the waters themselves, giving more than a strong hint of mineral richness, while the dark colour is set off against the bright red sandstone of the smooth-walled channels as it cuts into the riverbed.

Flows, forces, stoppers, and kettle holes. Weird formations and shapes etched into the delicate rock by the unyielding power of water. The power of the River Eden.

The Eden dashes past the old mill and castle at Armathwaite, then in its final stages mumbles along at a quite deceptive rate, by Wetheral and Warwick-on-Eden before plunging into the heart of Carlisle. Not far to go now, the river grinds over The Swifts as it gallops through Rickerby Park.

The tiny village of Rockcliffe overlooks the last bend in the river. Beyond this point, where the waters erode the banks of friable red and orange sandstone, the River Eden becomes the Solway Firth, one of the greatest estuaries in Britain.

Mudflats and merse are now all around, just below the village of Rockcliffe. Here there is a large nature reserve - Rockcliffe Marsh, managed by the Cumbria Wildlife Trust, and on the north side of the marsh, another great river floods the flatlands of the Solway basin, the River Esk.

A vastness of wild flat merse, broad and long, cutting into the mudflats of the estuary, Rockcliffe Marsh is arguably the most important nature reserve on the Firth. The marsh is flat, at first glance at least, for here the close-cropped turfs, sea-washed and saline, are bedded in silt brought down from the hills by the mighty rivers.

Rockcliffe Marsh is primarily a bird reserve, and is a good place to visit both in summer and in winter.

Summer on Rockcliffe Marsh is wonderful. As you approach the merse, skylarks and meadow pipits rise from their hidden cup-shaped nests, while lapwings, oystercatchers, redshanks, and ringed plovers also nest on the saltmarsh. However, the most obvious breeding birds here are gulls and terns. There is a huge colony of breeding herring gulls and lesser black-baked gulls, while common and Arctic terns also find room to lay their eggs in relative privacy.

It is because of these important numbers of breeding birds that access to Rockcliffe Marsh is by permit only during the summer months.

Winter is a very different kettle of fish at Rockcliffe, for then it is not that unusual for the entire Svalbard population of barnacle geese to descend on the merse - their numbers swelled by hundreds of pink-footed and greylag geese.

Hen harriers quarter the flats looking for food, and occasional peregrines dash by, putting up large flocks of dunlin or redshank.

This is the story of the great river. From its source to the sea. This book will take you on that journey, and hopefully will encourage some of you to visit Eden too.

**Graham Uney**
**2008**

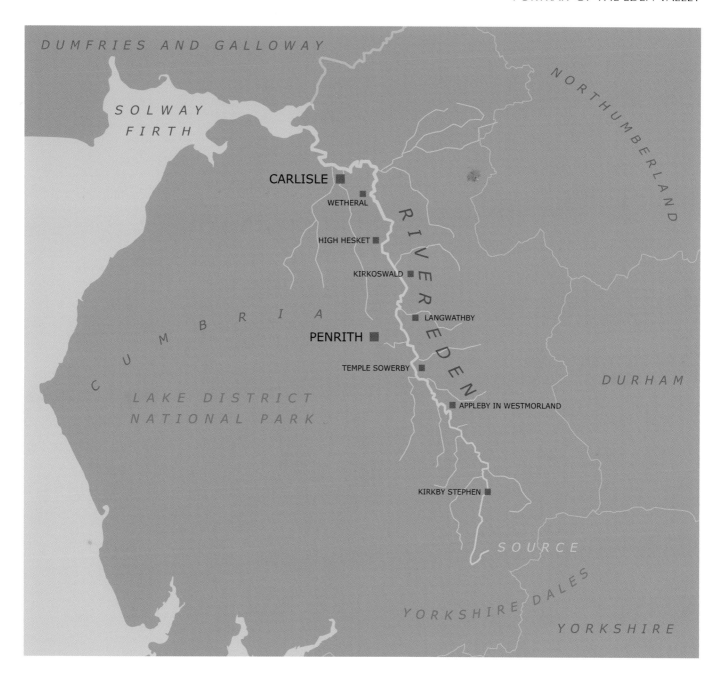

# ACKNOWLEDGEMENTS

*To Olivia, for sharing many happy times in the Eden Valley.*

*Thanks are due to Steven Pugsley at Halsgrove, and to the staff at Paramo for kitting me out in clothing to keep me warm and dry in all weathers whilst exploring the Eden. Thanks are also due to Julie Darroch and Nicola Hewitson of Cumbria Tourism for their assistance, and to the Appleby Manor Hotel for their hospitality.*

*The Eden Valley is that great and broad trench, sliced by the mighty river, between the rugged volcanic peaks of the Lake District and the rounded sediment layers of gritstone and limestone that form the Pennines.*

*At the head of the Eden Valley, the upper dale is known as Mallerstang.*
*Swarth Fell forms the western side to the dale.*

*A few scattered trees dot the moorland and rough pastures at the head of Mallerstang.*

*This is sheep farming country, and every field and pasture has its own byre. Above this one the broad slopes of Wild Boar Fell rise.*

Opposite
*The Eden begins its life high on Mallerstang Edge, on Hugh Seat, a peaty hill with little defining features. Once the infant river throws itself off Hellgill Force it turns north and starts to cut its trench towards the sea.*

*The Settle to Carlisle Railway line runs through the valley. Here above Hellgill an old railway shed stands among moorland hard rushes.*

*Open moorland slopes rise above a field barn to the summit flanks of Swarth Fell.*

*In the summer months the upper pastures are transformed into lush wildflower meadows, full of colour and life. Mallerstang Edge looks impressive here, etched dark between the sky and these vivid meadows.*

One of the many wild fell ponies that roam around the upper part of the Eden Valley.

On the high moors of Mallerstang, where heather grows in profusion, red grouse can often be seen. These gamebirds rely on heather – they eat the fresh shoots, and take shelter in older clumps.

*The two most common heather species growing together. Erica cinerea (Bell Heather) on the left,
and Calluna vulgaris (Ling) growing on the right.*

*Bright sunshine pierces the dark clouds above Wild Boar Fell.*

*The line of the Settle to Carlisle Railway can be seen cutting a straight
course above the pastures of Mallerstang.*

*Buttercup-filled meadows of Mallerstang, early in the morning. Each field is marked
out by ancient dry stone walls running up the fellside.*

*The stark limestone edge of Hangingstone Scar forms the rim of the moorland
plateau holding Hugh Seat and Archy Styrigg.*

*Early morning clouds roll down the dale in Mallerstang.*

*The River Eden bends through the pastures below Wild Boar Fell at the head of Mallerstang.*

*Most dry stone walls run straight up the fellside, but occasionally you are left wondering why on earth an odd bend was put in during the building process.*

*Thrang Bridge leads over the Eden to the farm at Deepgill.*

Pendragon Castle, legendary home of King Arthur, stands at the bottom of Mallerstang, where the dale widens beneath High Seat.

The River Eden at dawn, where Scotch Well Spring enters the river below Dalefoot.

Opposite
The village of Nateby is the first real village encountered as you head down the Eden Valley.

*In this rough land the sheep farmer has two aids –
his dog, and his quad bike. Like all collies, this dog is
always ready for a day in the hills.*

*The pass above Nateby is often closed by drifting snow
in the winter. It's just a single track linking the villages in
the Eden Valley to Birkdale at the head of Swaledale in
Yorkshire.*

*High Pike from Tailbridge Hill on Nateby Common.*

*Above Nateby the shepherd is out with his dog rounding up his flock.*

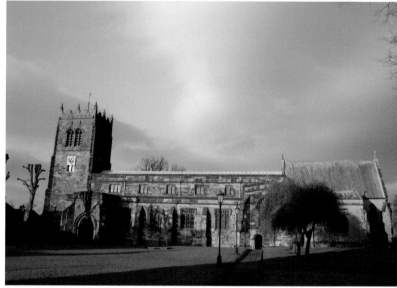

*The Cloisters in Kirkby Stephen, lies at the northern end of the market place, and is the entrance to the parish church.*

*The parish church of Kirkby Stephen, known locally as the Cathedral of the Dales, is built on the site on an old Saxon church and contains many ancient relics.*

*The Settle to Carlisle Railway is one of the main features of the Eden Valley.*
*Here the tracks run above the village of Crosby Garrett.*

*Harvest time in the hay meadows of the Eden Valley.*

*Limestone outcrops at various places around the Eden Valley. Here on Little Asby Scar there are small areas of limestone pavement.*

*Smardale Gill Viaduct curves its way across the narrow valley of Scandale Beck, 3 miles west of Kirkby Stephen. The viaduct has 14 arches, each with a 30 foot span, and a total length of 553 feet. The old track bed and the surrounding woodland is now managed as a nature reserve by the Cumbria Wildlife Trust.*

*A walker enjoying a stroll along the old railway through Smardale Gill.*

*Further downstream, the Hoff Beck joins the Eden at Colby near Appleby-in-Westmorland. Near the head of the Hoff Beck it plunges over Rutter Force beside an old mill.*

*Alongside the Hoff Beck is an exposed limestone face, known simply as The Hoff.*
*It is a popular place for rock climbing.*

*In the centre of Appleby-in-Westmorland the Moot Hall stands
by the market place.*

*A plaque on the side of the Moot Hall in
Appleby-in-Westmorland shows that the town's
heritage goes back at least as far as 1179.*

*Dufton is a typical little fellside village. It nestles beneath Dufton Pike, and the higher hills of Knock Fell and Meldon Hill.*

*St Cuthbert's church lies to the north of Dufton village. It was built in the late eighteenth century and replaces an earlier stone building dating back to 1293. Many of the miners who worked on the high fells above the Eden are buried in the churchyard here. The church is named after St Cuthbert whose body was carried across the North Pennines in 875 AD by monks from Lindisfarne who were attempting to flee the Vikings.*

*The evening light turns clouds salmon pink above the levels of Brackenber Flodders.*

*Great Dun Fell with its coating of winter snow, from Bleacarn Tarn.*

*Frost clothes the fields beneath Knock Pike.*

*Beneath the western flank of Great Dun Fell, with its summit radar station gleaming white in the wintry sunlight, winter wheat pushes through frosty ground in the arable fields of the Eden Valley.*

*A light dusting of snow on the higher tops of the North Pennines. Here Great Dun Fell and Little Dun Fell rise above the village of Milburn.*

*At Kirkland the old church of St Lawrence lies beneath the western slopes of Cross Fell.*

*The wild landscape of the Moor House National Nature Reserve above the head of Teesdale.*

*A walker on the Pennine Way strides out towards Great Dun Fell.*

*From the top of Little Dun Fell, with its tiny summit cairn, the dome of Great Dun Fell's summit radar station dominates the view.*

*The summit of Great Dun Fell is scarred by the white dome of a radar station. The highest point of the hill is within the private grounds of the station.*

*The peaty upland bogs of Great Dun Fell, looking north along the chain
towards Little Dun Fell and distant Cross Fell.*

Opposite
*The Pennine Way passes over the tops of the three highest summits of the Pennines - Cross Fell, Great Dun
Fell, and Little Dun Fell. The huge numbers of walkers taking on the challenge of this superb long distance
trail lead to erosion of the moorland peat beds. Much of the route now has paving slabs laid to protect
the moorland. This is the section from Tees Head towards Little Dun Fell. These fells fall away to the Eden
Valley to the west.*

*On the flanks of Little Dun Fell, overlooking the Crowdundle Beck which flows into the Eden below Acorn Bank, the rocks of Middle Tongue form a rough scree slope leading down to the valley.*

*As you approach the summit plateau of Cross Fell, the highest mountain of the whole Pennine chain, the rough screes above Tees Head lead the eye eastwards across the rough moors of the North Pennines Area of Outstanding Natural Beauty.*

*Cross Fell from Tees Head.*

*On the south-eastern rim of the Cross Fell summit plateau stands a lone stone currick.*

*The northern fringes of the Cross Fell summit plateau has this
large cairn marking the route down The Screes.*

*A walker heading for Little Dun Fell and Great Dun Fell from the summit plateau of Cross Fell.*

*Adders are common the moors of the Pennines, particularly around bouldery slopes which provide shelter as well as warmth as the rocks radiate heat.*

Opposite
*Cross Fell in winter, looking impregnable from near Langwathby.*

*To the north of Cross Fell the wild moors continue. There is a high road pass, taken by the A686 from the Eden Valley over to Alston in Tynedale, and from the summit of this pass at Hartside, Cross Fell looks a long way off.*

*An old shepherd's cottage by the roadside on the way up to Hartside Height from the Eden Valley. The moors of Black Fell and Watch Hill roll away to the north.*

*Black grouse are rare moorland birds. They have been in serious decline here in the North Pennines for a number of years, as they have elsewhere in Scotland and in Wales. However, over recent years the North Pennine population has seen a bit of a recovery.*

*St Michael's church stands within an extensive churchyard in Lowther Park on the west side of the Eden Valley, on the fringes of the Lake District National Park.*

*Inside St Michael's church at Lowther.*

*A cross in the churchyard at Lowther, on the west side of the Eden Valley.*

*In the churchyard at Lowther Park is the mausoleum of William, the Second Earl of Lowther, who died in 1844. Inside the mausoleum there is a statue of the Earl sitting in gloomy isolation.*

*Acorn Bank sits by the Crowdundle Beck, just before it flows into the River Eden. It's a grand old house, which sadly is not open to the public. However, the National Trust, which owns the house, has maintained a lovely old orchard and herb garden, which you can visit.*

*Inside the herb garden at Acorn Bank.*

*The orchards at Acorn Bank hold many rare and unusual apple varieties. The National Trust also holds an Apple Day here each October, which is great fun.*

*The current Brougham Castle (pronounced 'broom') stands on the site of a Roman fortress. It overlooks the River Eamont on the outskirts of Penrith, just before the river enters the Eden.*

*Although much of Brougham Castle is now in ruins, it is well worth exploring.*

Opposite
*A doorway leading into one of the towers at Brougham Castle.*

*An old cross in the churchyard at Brougham.*

*Brougham church is a lovely squat old building, of Penrith fell sandstone.*

*On the fringes of the Lake District National Park, where the Northern Fells fall eastwards into the subsidiary valleys that run into the Eden, lovely open meadows and moor clothe the slopes of the low hills. This is Calebreck, on the slopes of Carrock Fell.*

*The charming village of Hesket Newmarket, a one-time hub for miners working the seams and adits within the Northern Fells of the Lake District National Park.*

Opposite
*Above Calebreck, on the slopes of Carrock Fell, a footpath sign invites you to explore the open access land of Caldbeck Common.*

*Walking down from off the Northern Fells of the Lake District National Park towards the village of Hesket Newmarket.*

*Below Carrock Fell the hay meadows are harvested to provide fodder for livestock.*

Opposite
*The River Caldew flowing at Water's Meet below Hesket Newmarket.*

*Exploring the lovely woodlands of the River Caldew. The river is a major tributary of the Eden, and drains the high peaks of Carrock Fell, Bowscale Fell, and Skiddaw in the Lake District National Park.*

*Wonderful old cottages, their gardens dropping down to the banks of the River Caldew, in Caldbeck village.*

*Caldbeck is a peaceful little village in the valley of the River Caldew.*

*The churchyard at Caldbeck, final resting place of the great huntsman John Peel.*

*Rolling farmland is typical of the landscape around the Caldew where it flows north-eastwards to join the River Eden.*

*The River Eden north of Penrith is a much wider waterway. It now takes the water from a number of major rivers, flowing onwards to the Solway Firth.*

*The ancient standing stone of Long Meg near Langwathby.*

*At Long Meg Standing Stone there is an ancient circle of lesser stones, known as Long Meg's Daughters.*

*All of the villages of the lower Eden Valley have houses primarily built of red sandstone. This is the main street through Kirkoswald.*

*The old market cross and the Fetherstone Arms in Kirkoswald.*

*On a hill just south of Kirkoswald stands this folly.*

Opposite
*The church at Kirkoswald lies in the meadows beneath the village,
overlooking the River Eden.*

*Eden Bridge in winter, on the minor road between Kirkoswald and Lazonby.*

*Head a little further north along the Eden and you come to Armathwaite. Here there is an impressive old castle, and a bridge spanning the river.*

*Otters are common throughout the River Eden, although being largely nocturnal they are seen infrequently.*

*East of the Eden, where the Pennine chain drops towards the Scottish border, the open moors of Geltsdale are now managed as a nature reserve by the RSPB.*

Opposite
*An old shooting lodge, known as The Gairs, high on the moors of Geltsdale.*

*At the entrance to the higher part of Geltsdale there is a small hill overlooking the flatlands of the Solway Firth. This is Talkin Fell.*

Opposite
*Geltsdale at dusk from The Green.*

*The road down to the Solway, off Talkin Fell.*

*The northern extremes of the Pennines, Cold Fell above Forest Head.*

*On the northern slopes of Cold Fell the RSPB manage a large segment of moorland, as well as hay meadows and the open water of Tindale Tarn.*

*Exploring the RSPB Reserve at Tindale Tarn.*

*The wonderfully wild moorland of Cold Fell rises above the wildflower meadows of Tindale.*

*Yellow Rattle, one of the more common plants of the wildflower meadows of the North Pennines.*

*Buttercups as far as the eye can see at Tindale.*

*Tindale Tarn, at the northern end of the Pennines.*

*The tiny village of Tindale is an old mining community.*

*Above Brampton lies the Ridgewood with its network of paths leading through lovely dappled woodland.*

Opposite
*Brampton is a charming little market town on the fringes of the Pennines.*

The 'modern' town of Brampton now lies away from the river, but the old town was much nearer. Now there's just a farm and the old church alongside the River Irthing, a tributary of the Eden.

The old church at Brampton.

Opposite
A little further east along the River Irthing there is a small side stream known as the Quarry Beck. It has a number of little waterfalls along its length.

*Quarry Beck running through woodland down to Lanercost Priory on the Irthing.*

*Naworth Castle, just east of Brampton, in autumn. Naworth was the one-time home of Belted Will. Lord William Howard was born in 1563, and became nicknamed Belted Will by Sir Walter Scott in his poem 'Lay of the Last Minstrel'.*

*Lanercost Priory was founded about 1166 by Henry II. It stands by the lovely River Irthing just north-east of Brampton.*

Opposite
*Lanercost Priory from Abbey Bridge*

*Abbey Bridge over the River Irthing at Lanercost.*

*Lanercost Priory is open to visitors, and is worth exploring.*

*Back on the Eden Wetheral Priory Gatehouse is a superb building laying just above the river. It is the fifteenth-century gatehouse of a Benedictine priory, where wrongdoers could claim pardon if they enlisted to fight against the Scots.*

Opposite
*Abbey Bridge at Lanercost.*

*The church at Wetheral, just above the river, is built of red sandstone.*

*Hay meadows being harvested at Wetheral, beside the River Eden.*

*A sleeping farm dog near the village of Hayton.*

*On the west side of the River Eden, before the river enters Carlisle, lies the red stone ramparts of Rose Castle near Dalston. This is the palace of the Bishop of Carlisle, although it is not open to the public.*

*On the edge of Carlisle, in the Rickerby area just by the Eden, lies an octagonal Victorian folly tower erected by George Head.*

Carlisle Castle guards the western end of the border between England and Scotland. William II built the first timber castle at Carlisle in 1092, and thirty years later his brother, King Henry I, ordered the building of a castle in stone which included the keep that now remains as the oldest part of the castle. It overlooks the River Eden on the north side of the city.


Opposite
The Carlisle Cursing Stone was installed at the city's Tullie House Museum in 2001. Since then the city has been affected by the worst floods in history, and factories have been destroyed by major fires. Foot and mouth disease has decimated livestock in the vicinity, and there has been a marked increase in local unemployment. Perhaps worst of all though, Carlisle United soccer team dropped to a lower league! Many local people feel the stone should be destroyed.

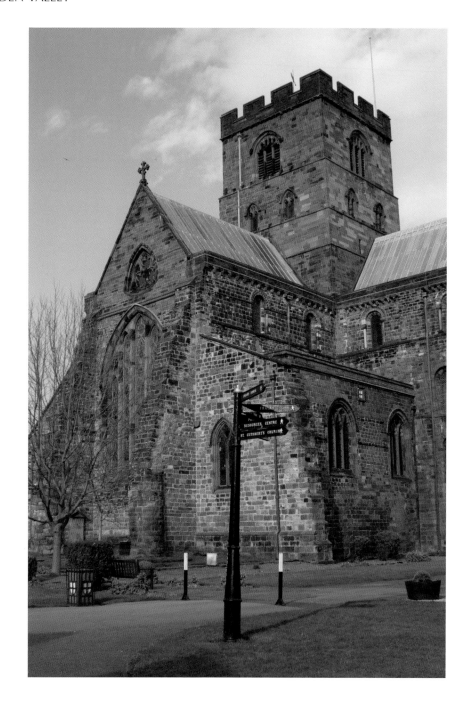

*The sculpture 'Global Warming' by Anthony Turner stands on the village green at Rockcliffe. The River Eden flows by behind, just before it enters the wider Solway Basin.*

Opposite
*Carlisle Cathedral was built in 1122 and stands at the very centre of the city, not far from the banks of the Eden.*

*A road sign at Easton on the banks of the Solway
Firth, the open merse behind.*

*Rippled sand where the River Eden joins the Solway.*

142

*King Edward 1st monument on Burgh Marsh where the River Eden becomes the Solway Firth.*

*Barnacle geese flying in to the Solway Basin from their summer nesting grounds on Svalbard in the Arctic.*